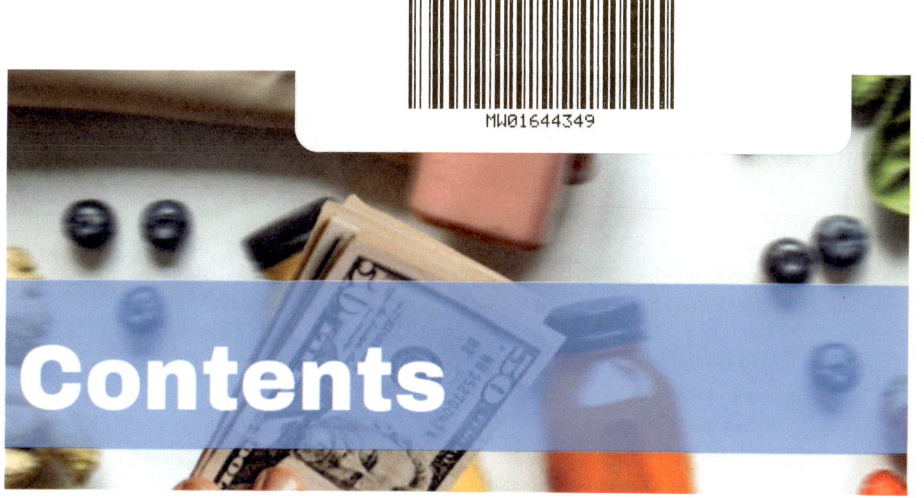

Contents

Introduction 3

- Explanation of the purpose of the book
- The importance of budgeting
- The benefits of learning how to budget

Getting started with budgeting...6

- Why you should create a budget
- How to calculate your income
- How to track your expenses

Creating a budget 11

- Determining your essential expenses
- Budgeting for non-essential expenses
- Saving for emergencies

Managing your budget 18

- Tips for sticking to your budget
- How to adjust your budget when necessary
- Planning for long-term financial goals

Maximizing your paycheck 26

- Understanding your paycheck and taxes
- Strategies for increasing your income
- Saving for retirement

Conclusion 34

- Final thoughts on budgeting
- Encouragement to continue budgeting

Forward

Are you ready to take control of your financial future? To kickstart a life of prosperity and freedom? Then this book is for you! I was once like you, fresh out of school and starting my first real job with no idea how to manage my newfound income. I made mistakes, I overspent, and I struggled. But I learned from those mistakes and through budgeting, I've transformed my financial life. And now, I want to share that knowledge with you.

Paycheck Detox is not your typical financial advice book filled with jargon and complicated formulas. It's a short, easy-to-read guide that will show you how to take control of your finances and set yourself up for a life of success. This is intended for young adults who don't have that support and guidance that we all need. From setting achievable financial goals to tracking your spending and building your savings, this book will walk you through every step of the budgeting process.

But this book is about more than just budgeting. It's about taking control of your future and realizing your dreams. By learning the value of consistency, discipline, and delayed gratification, you'll be able to turn small steps into giant leaps in more than just your finances. Just look at the inspiring stories of people like Oprah Winfrey, Steve Jobs, and J.K. Rowling - they started from humble beginnings and through hard work and perseverance, they achieved greatness.

So, are you ready to start your journey to financial freedom? Are you ready to detox your paycheck and unlock your potential? Then let's get started!

Peace and Power,

Introduction

Imagine this: you're a freshly-minted college grad, ready to take on the world and make your mark. You've landed your first real job, and you're feeling pretty good about yourself. You can finally afford to splurge on the things you've been dreaming about - new clothes, fancy dinners, and maybe even a sweet ride. But before you know it, reality sets in. You've got bills to pay, groceries to buy, and friends who want to go out every night of the week. You're not sure how you're going to make it all work, and the stress is starting to get to you.

That's where this book comes in. It's your roadmap to financial success, your guide to navigating the treacherous waters of budgeting and money management. With its easy-to-follow tips and strategies, you can avoid the common pitfalls that trip up so many young professionals, and start building a solid financial foundation for yourself. So whether you want to save up for that dream vacation, buy your first house, or retire early and travel the world, this book has got you covered. Don't let the stress of financial uncertainty hold you back - take control of your money, and start living the life you've always dreamed of!

The importance of budgeting

Meet Alex, a recent college graduate who just landed a job as a marketing executive at a top advertising agency. Alex is excited to start earning a steady income and finally be able to afford some of the things he's always wanted. But as the first paycheck comes in, Alex is hit with a realization - he has no idea how to manage his money.

He decides to turn to a book on budgeting, hoping it will help him get his finances in order. As he reads through the chapters, he realizes the importance of having a budget and sticking to it. He learns how to create a budget by calculating his income, listing his expenses, and prioritizing his spending.

Alex also learns about the importance of sticking to his budget. He realizes that if he doesn't control his spending, he'll end up living paycheck to paycheck and won't be able to save for the future. He also learns about common budgeting mistakes to avoid, like underestimating expenses or being too inflexible with his budget.

As he finishes the book, Alex feels confident that he can create a budget that will help him achieve his financial goals. He knows that by prioritizing his spending and sticking to his budget, he can avoid debt and build up an emergency fund. He's also excited to start saving for the future, whether it's for a dream vacation or an early retirement.

Alex feels grateful for the advice and guidance provided in the book. He knows that budgeting isn't always easy, but with the right mindset and strategies, he can achieve financial stability and peace of mind.

The benefits of learning how to budget

After Alex had created his budget, he noticed a significant change in his financial situation. He was no longer living paycheck to paycheck and had money left over at the end of each month. He had a better understanding of his expenses and knew exactly how much money he could spend without going over budget.

But the benefits of budgeting didn't stop there. Alex realized that he was becoming more disciplined with his spending habits. He was no longer making impulsive purchases or splurging on unnecessary items. He had set clear financial goals for himself, and he was determined to stick to them.

As he continued to track his expenses and stick to his budget, Alex noticed that he was able to save more money than he ever had before. He started to build up an emergency fund, which gave him peace of mind knowing that he had money set aside for unexpected expenses. He also started to invest his money in a retirement account, which he knew would pay off in the long run.

But perhaps the most significant benefit of learning how to budget was the sense of control it gave Alex over his financial future. He no longer felt helpless when it came to money. Instead, he had a plan in place and felt confident that he could achieve his financial goals.

Alex was grateful for the guidance and advice provided in the book that had helped him learn how to budget. He knew that he still had a lot to learn, but he was determined to continue to educate himself on personal finance and investing. He was excited about the future and the possibilities it held, knowing that he had the tools and knowledge to make the most of his money.

Getting started with budgeting

- Track your income and expenses to understand your spending habits.
- Use a budget spreadsheet or app to organize expenses.
- Cut back on spending or increase earnings where possible (e.g. eat out less, reduce entertainment expenses).
- Set realistic savings goals and create a plan.
- Prepare for unexpected expenses.
- Check progress regularly and adjust the budget as needed.

The benefits of learning how to budget

Alex decided to create a budget for a few reasons. The first reason was that he was tired of living paycheck to paycheck. He had been working for a few months now and was frustrated that he didn't have any money left over at the end of the month. He knew that he needed to take control of his finances if he wanted to have any chance of saving money and building wealth.

The second reason was that he had some unexpected expenses come up recently that had thrown his finances into disarray. He had to take his car to the shop for repairs, and the cost was much higher than he had anticipated. He also had a medical bill that he hadn't budgeted for, and it had left him scrambling to make ends meet.

If Alex hadn't decided to create a budget, things could have turned out much worse for him. He could have continued to live paycheck to paycheck, constantly struggling to make ends meet. He might have had to take on debt to cover unexpected expenses or to pay for things he couldn't afford.

Without a budget, Alex would have been at the mercy of his finances, never knowing where his money was going or how much he could afford to spend. He might have missed out on opportunities to invest in his future or to help out his family in times of need.

But thanks to his decision to create a budget, Alex was able to take control of his finances and start building a better future for himself. He knew that there would still be challenges ahead, but he was confident that he had the tools and knowledge to overcome them.

How to calculate your income

Alex started by calculating his monthly income, which included his take-home pay from his job and any additional income he received (such as freelance work or side gigs). To calculate his take-home pay, he used the following formula:

Take-Home Pay = Gross Pay - Deductions

For example, if Alex's gross pay (before taxes and other deductions) was $3,000 per month, and his deductions (such as taxes, Social Security, and retirement contributions) totaled $800 per month, his take-home pay would be:

Take-Home Pay = $3,000 - $800 = $2,200 per month

Once Alex had calculated his take-home pay, he added up all of his sources of income (including any additional income from freelance work or side gigs) to get his total monthly income.

To calculate your total monthly income, start by adding up all of your sources of income. If you have a regular salary or wages, this will be the easiest part of the calculation. If you have additional sources of income (such as freelance work or side gigs), be sure to include those as well.

Remember that your income can vary from month to month, so it's important to keep track of all of your sources of income and make adjustments to your budget as needed. By starting with a clear understanding of your monthly income, you'll be able to make smarter financial decisions and stay on track with your financial goals.

How to track your expenses

Alex knew that in order to keep his budget in check, he needed to track his expenses. He tried different tools, including a simple notebook where he jotted down his purchases, and even created a spreadsheet on his computer.

But, as he started earning more and his expenses increased, Alex realized that he needed a more efficient method. He did some research and found some great resources that made tracking his expenses a breeze.

One of the tools he found was an app that connected to his bank account and automatically categorized his spending. This made it easier for him to see where his money was going and identify areas where he needed to cut back.

Another option he used was a budgeting software that allowed him to create a customized spending plan and track his progress throughout the month. This gave him a better understanding of his spending habits and helped him adjust his budget accordingly.

Alex also learned some useful formulas and calculations to help him track his expenses. He used the "50/30/20" rule, where he allocated 50% of his income to necessities, 30% to discretionary spending, and 20% to savings and debt repayment. He also calculated his debt-to-income ratio, which helped him determine if he was taking on too much debt.

By using these tools and calculations, Alex was able to stay on top of his expenses and make smarter financial decisions. He even noticed that he had some extra money left over at the end of each month, which he was able to put towards his savings goals.

How to track your expenses continued...

The bottom line is that tracking your expenses doesn't have to be complicated. With the right tools and formulas, you can stay on top of your spending and achieve your financial goals.

The "50/30/20" rule is like dividing up a pizza pie into three slices. Imagine you have a big pizza pie and you want to share it with two of your friends. You want to make sure everyone gets a fair share of the pizza, right? So you divide the pizza into three slices. The first slice, or 50%, is for your needs, like food, shelter, and clothing. The second slice, or 30%, is for your wants, like movies, clothes, and toys. And the last slice, or 20%, is for your savings, like putting money in your piggy bank or a savings account at the bank. By dividing the pizza pie fairly, you can enjoy your slice of pizza and save some for later too!

Creating a budget

Here is a basic outline to get started.

- **Determine Your Income:** Calculate your monthly income and write it down.
- **Track Your Expenses:** Keep track of all your expenses for a month and categorize them.
- **Identify Your Essential Expenses:** Determine your essential expenses such as rent, utilities, groceries, transportation, and any other necessary expenses.
- **Determine Your Discretionary Expenses:** Review your tracked expenses and identify areas where you can cut back. These may include eating out, entertainment, shopping, and other non-essential expenses.
- **Create Your Budget:** Using the 50/30/20 rule or another budgeting method, allocate your income to your essential and discretionary expenses, as well as savings and debt repayment.

Determining your essential expenses

As Alex continued with his budgeting journey, he knew that he needed to identify his essential expenses. He started by looking at his bank statements and credit card bills from the past few months. He then separated his expenses into two categories: essential and non-essential.

Alex's essential expenses included his rent, utilities, groceries, transportation, and minimum debt payments. These were the expenses that he needed to pay every month in order to survive and maintain his current lifestyle. For example, he needed to pay his rent to have a place to live and his utility bills to have electricity and water.

Next, Alex took a closer look at his essential expenses and calculated the total cost. He used a simple formula: adding up all of his expenses from each category and subtracting that amount from his total income. This helped him understand how much of his income was being spent on essential expenses.

Once he knew how much he was spending on essential expenses, Alex was able to set a realistic budget for himself. He knew that he needed to allocate a certain portion of his income towards these expenses every month in order to cover them.

As Alex continued to track his expenses, he found that it was helpful to review his essential expenses on a regular basis. This allowed him to identify any areas where he might be overspending and make adjustments as needed.

Determining your essential expenses continued...

By understanding his essential expenses and setting a budget, Alex was able to take control of his finances and make informed decisions about his spending. He knew that he was on the right track towards achieving his financial goals and creating a secure future for himself.

Here's an example of how Alex created a list of his essential expenses:

- He started by making a list of his regular monthly bills, like rent, utilities, and phone bills.
- He then added other necessary expenses like groceries, transportation, and medical expenses.
- Alex also included any debt payments, such as credit card bills and student loans.
- He made sure to prioritize expenses that were necessary for his daily living and survival.

To help visualize his expenses, Alex created a table with four columns:

Expense	Due Date	Amount Due	Paid
Rent	1st of the month	$800	Yes
Utilities	15th of the month	$150	No
Groceries	Weekly	$100	No
Transportation	Monthly	$75	Yes
Credit Card	Monthly	$50	No

Budgeting for non-essential expenses

Alex sat down at his desk with a cup of coffee and started reviewing his tracked expenses. He had already identified his essential expenses, but now he needed to determine his discretionary expenses. He knew that these were the areas where he could cut back and save some money.

As he looked through his expenses, he noticed that he spent a lot of money on eating out. He loved trying new restaurants and meeting up with friends for meals, but he realized that it was costing him a lot of money. He decided to limit himself to eating out only once a week and to cook the rest of his meals at home.

Next, he looked at his entertainment expenses. He loved going to concerts and movies, but he knew that these were non-essential expenses that he could cut back on. He decided to limit himself to one concert or movie per month and to look for free or low-cost events to attend instead.

Finally, he looked at his shopping expenses. He realized that he had a habit of buying new clothes and gadgets even when he didn't really need them. He decided to limit himself to one new item per month and to start selling or donating items that he no longer used.

To keep track of his discretionary expenses, Alex created a separate category in his budget spreadsheet. He labeled it "Non-Essential Expenses" and included subcategories for eating out, entertainment, and shopping. He set a monthly budget for each subcategory and made sure to stick to it.

Budgeting for non-essential expenses continued...

As he started to cut back on his non-essential expenses, Alex began to see a difference in his finances. He was able to save more money and put it towards his goals, such as building an emergency fund and paying off his student loans. He also felt more in control of his spending and less stressed about his finances.

Alex knew that determining his discretionary expenses and tracking them was a crucial step in budgeting. He realized that by making small changes and being mindful of his spending, he could achieve his financial goals and live a more fulfilling life within his means.

Here is a simple table that Alex used to track his discretionary expenses:

Date	Category	Amount	Notes
1/1/2023	Eating Out	$25.00	Lunch with co-workers
1/3/2023	Entertainment	$20.00	Movie ticket
1/4/2023	Shopping	$50.00	New pair of shoes
1/5/2023	Eating Out	$30.00	Dinner with friends
1/7/2023	Entertainment	$15.00	Video game purchase
1/8/2023	Eating Out	$40.00	Brunch with family

Using a table like this can make it easy to quickly see where your money is going and identify areas where you can cut back. Additionally, Alex used a budgeting app on his phone to help him track his expenses on the go. The app allowed him to set spending limits for different categories and send him notifications when he was close to reaching his limit. This helped him stay accountable and make better spending decisions.

Saving for emergencies

Alex had now been budgeting for a few months, and he felt like he had a good handle on his essential and discretionary expenses. But one thing he hadn't accounted for was emergencies.

He realized that unexpected events, like car repairs or medical bills, could easily throw off his budget and put him in a tough spot. So, he decided to set aside some money each month for emergencies.

First, he made a list of potential emergency expenses, like car repairs, medical bills, or unexpected travel. Then, he estimated how much he would need to cover each expense. Based on this, he decided to set aside $100 each month for emergencies.

But he also wanted to find ways to save even more without drastically cutting back on his current spending. So, he did some research and found some simple ways to skim a little money off his spending.

For example, he started using cashback apps and websites when shopping online. He also canceled subscriptions he didn't use and negotiated his bills with service providers to save a few extra dollars each month.

Alex was proud of himself for taking these steps to prepare for the unexpected. He knew that emergencies could happen to anyone, and having a plan in place would give him peace of mind.

Saving for emergencies continued...

Now, he felt confident that he had a solid budget in place that would help him achieve his financial goals while still enjoying his life.

Here is an example chart for Alex's emergency fund and how he tracked his expenses:

Category	Budgeted Amount	Actual Amount	Difference
Emergency Fund	$1,000	$500	$500
Car Repairs	$100	$0	$100
Medical Expenses	$50	$75	-$25
Home Repairs	$50	$0	$50
Total	$1,200	$575	$625

In this chart, the first column lists the different categories of expenses and the budgeted amount for each. The second column shows the actual amount that Alex spent in each category. The third column calculates the difference between the budgeted amount and the actual amount, which helps Alex identify areas where he may need to adjust his budget.

The emergency fund category is separate from other expenses and serves as a cushion for unexpected events. In this example, Alex budgeted $1,000 for his emergency fund but has only saved $500 so far. He also budgeted specific amounts for car repairs, medical expenses, and home repairs, but has not yet spent any money on car or home repairs. However, he did spend more than he budgeted on medical expenses.

By tracking his expenses in this way, Alex can better manage his budget and prepare for unexpected events without dipping into his regular spending money.

Managing your budget

1. **Review your budget regularly** - Check your budget on a regular basis, such as once a month, to see if you're staying on track.

2. **Adjust as needed** - Make adjustments to your budget as necessary to accommodate changes in income, expenses, or financial goals.

3. **Track your spending** - Keep track of your spending throughout the month to ensure you're sticking to your budget.

4. **Identify areas for improvement** - Look for areas where you can cut back on expenses to save more money.

5. **Automate savings** - Set up automatic transfers to savings accounts to make it easier to save money each month.

Managing your budget means keeping track of the money you have and the money you spend. This is important because it helps you make sure you have enough money for the things you need and want, and it helps you avoid spending too much money and getting into debt.

Tips for sticking to your budget

Set a realistic budget: Determine your income and expenses, and create a budget that is feasible for you. For example, if your income is $2,500 a month and your essential expenses total $1,500, you may decide to allocate $500 for discretionary spending and $500 for savings.

Use a budgeting app or spreadsheet: There are many apps and templates available to help you track your spending and stay on budget. For example, apps like Mint or YNAB can link to your accounts and categorize your spending automatically.

Monitor your spending: Check your bank and credit card statements regularly to make sure you're sticking to your budget. If you find that you're overspending in a particular category, adjust your budget accordingly.

Cut back on non-essential expenses: Identify areas where you can reduce your spending, such as eating out, entertainment, or shopping. For example, you may decide to cook at home instead of eating out, or watch a movie at home instead of going to the theater.

Set goals and track your progress: Whether it's saving for a down payment on a house or paying off student loans, set specific goals and track your progress. For example, if your goal is to save $5,000 in a year, break it down into monthly increments and track how much you save each month.

Avoid impulse purchases: Before making a purchase, take a moment to ask yourself if it's a necessary expense or an impulse buy. For example, if you're considering buying a new pair of shoes, think about whether you really need them or if it's just a want.

Use cash for discretionary spending: Using cash for discretionary spending can help you stick to your budget and avoid overspending. For example, if you've allocated $100 for entertainment for the month, withdraw $100 in cash and only use that for entertainment expenses.

Plan ahead for larger expenses: If you know you have a larger expense coming up, such as a car repair or a vacation, plan for it in advance and set aside money each month to cover the cost.

Tips for sticking to your budget continued...

Take advantage of coupons and discounts: Look for coupons and discounts when making purchases to save money. For example, you may use a coupon code when shopping online, or clip coupons from a newspaper for groceries.

Don't be too hard on yourself: Remember that budgeting is a learning process, and it's okay if you make mistakes or overspend occasionally. Just adjust your budget and keep working towards your financial goals.

Alex had been budgeting for a while, and he was starting to get the hang of it. He knew that sticking to a budget was key to reaching his financial goals, but it wasn't always easy. Sometimes, he would get tempted to spend money on things he didn't really need. However, he had a few tricks up his sleeve to help him stay on track.

One of the things Alex did was to set specific goals for his money. For example, he wanted to save up for a down payment on a house. Whenever he was tempted to make an unnecessary purchase, he would remind himself of his goal and ask himself if the purchase was worth delaying his dream of owning a home. This helped him prioritize his spending and stay focused on his long-term goals.

Another trick Alex used was to automate his savings. He set up a direct deposit to transfer a portion of his paycheck into a separate savings account each month. This way, he didn't have to think about saving money, it was already done for him. He could still enjoy his day-to-day spending without worrying about whether he was putting enough aside for his future.

Alex also made use of technology to help him track his spending. He downloaded a budgeting app on his phone, which allowed him to see all his transactions in one place. He could easily categorize his spending and see where his money was going. This helped him identify areas where he could cut back and stay within his budget.

Finally, Alex knew that he needed to be flexible with his budget. Life can be unpredictable, and unexpected expenses can arise. He made sure to include a buffer in his budget for these types of situations. This way, he wouldn't have to dip into his savings or go into debt to cover an unexpected expense.

Tips for sticking to your budget continued...

Overall, Alex's tips for sticking to a budget were:

- Set specific goals for your money to help prioritize spending.
- Automate your savings to make sure you're putting money aside each month.
- Use technology to track your spending and identify areas where you can cut back.
- Include a buffer in your budget for unexpected expenses.

By following these tips, Alex was able to stick to his budget and make progress towards his financial goals.

When it comes to sticking with your budget, it's important to understand the concept of opportunity cost. Essentially, every time you spend money on something, you're giving up the opportunity to spend that money on something else. It's important to weigh the cost of each purchase against what you could be doing with that money instead. For example, let's say you love riding go-karts and it costs you $40 each time you go.

Now you're considering buying tickets to a show that cost $120, but for $40 more, you can get a better location. While it may seem like a good deal, it's important to consider the opportunity cost. That $40 could be spent on three go-kart rides, something you really enjoy. By understanding the true cost of each purchase, you'll be better equipped to make decisions that align with your budget and financial goals.

In summary, correlating similar priced items and opportunities can help you stick to your budget by allowing you to make informed decisions on how to allocate your money. It helps you to weigh the cost of a purchase against your financial priorities, such as saving for a future goal or paying off debt.

By being mindful of your spending and making deliberate choices, you can avoid impulse buys and stay within your budget. These tips are useful because they provide practical strategies for staying on track financially and building healthy money habits for the long term.

How to adjust your budget when necessary

Alex had been following his budget for a few months now, and everything seemed to be going well. But one day, he received a call from his landlord that his apartment needed some urgent repairs. The repairs were going to cost him a significant amount of money, and he realized that he had not accounted for such expenses in his budget.

Feeling overwhelmed, Alex took a deep breath and decided to reassess his budget. He knew he had to adjust it to account for the unexpected expense.

The first thing Alex did was to review his budget to identify areas where he could cut back. He realized he had been spending more on eating out and entertainment than he needed to. So, he decided to cut back on those expenses and put the money towards the repairs.

Alex also looked at his savings account to see if he had enough to cover the cost of the repairs. Fortunately, he had been saving a small portion of his paycheck each month, and he had built up a decent emergency fund. He decided to use some of the money from his emergency fund to pay for the repairs.

Alex also decided to explore other options to reduce the cost of the repairs. He contacted a few repair companies and got different quotes. After comparing the prices, he was able to negotiate with one of the companies to lower the cost of the repairs.

Overall, Alex was able to adjust his budget and handle the unexpected expense without going into debt. He learned that being flexible and adaptable with his budget was crucial in times of unexpected expenses.

Here are some tips on how to adjust your budget when necessary:

- Review your budget and identify areas to cut back on discretionary expenses.
- Use your emergency fund to cover unexpected expenses. If you don't have one, start building one.
- Negotiate to reduce costs when faced with unexpected expenses.
- Be flexible and willing to adjust your budget when necessary to accommodate unexpected expenses or changes in your financial situation.

How to adjust your budget when necessary continued...

Cut back on non-essential spending. Use your emergency fund if you have one, or start building one by saving a little each month. Negotiate to lower costs and be willing to adjust your budget as needed.

Prioritize Essential Expenses: Prioritizing essential expenses means paying the bills and allocating funds towards necessary items such as groceries and transportation. For example, Alex would always make sure that he paid his rent and utilities first before spending money on other things like entertainment or shopping.

Review Discretionary Expenses: To review discretionary expenses, Alex would track all his non-essential spending such as eating out, entertainment, and shopping. He would then evaluate if there were any areas where he could cut back on spending. For instance, if he noticed that he was spending too much money on eating out, he would try to cook more meals at home to save money.

Budget for Emergencies: Alex made sure to set aside a portion of his income towards an emergency fund in case unexpected expenses came up. For example, if his car broke down, he would have the money saved to pay for the repair.

Adjust the Budget When Necessary: Alex understood that life is unpredictable, and sometimes he needed to adjust his budget to accommodate unexpected expenses. For instance, if he had to take time off work due to an illness, he would adjust his budget to ensure he could cover his essential expenses without dipping into his emergency fund.

Use Technology to Help: Alex utilized technology to help him manage his budget. He would use budgeting apps and online banking tools to track his expenses and stay within his budget. For example, he would set up automatic transfers to his emergency fund every month to ensure he was consistently saving for emergencies.

Be Mindful of Credit Card Spending: Alex was mindful of his credit card spending and understood the importance of paying off his balance in full every month to avoid interest charges. He would also only use his credit card for essential expenses and emergencies. For example, he would use his credit card to pay for a car repair but not for an impulse buy at the mall.

By following these tips, Alex was able to successfully manage his budget and avoid unnecessary financial stress.

Planning for long-term financial goals

Alex understood that building wealth is a gradual process and requires long-term planning. To plan for his long-term financial goals, he followed these steps:

Set clear financial goals: Alex set specific, measurable, achievable, relevant, and time-bound (SMART) financial goals. He identified what he wanted to achieve, when he wanted to achieve it, and how much money he needed to achieve it.

Prioritize his goals: Alex ranked his goals in order of importance and created a plan to achieve them one by one. He focused on his most important goal first and made sure he had a solid plan in place to achieve it before moving on to the next.

Create a realistic budget: Alex created a budget that accounted for his income, expenses, and savings. He made sure to allocate a portion of his income towards his long-term goals, while still allowing himself some flexibility for unexpected expenses or leisure activities.

Maximize his income: Alex looked for ways to increase his income by taking on a part-time job or starting a side hustle. He used the extra income to accelerate his progress towards his long-term goals.

Invest for the long-term: Alex understood that investing in the stock market and other financial markets was a long-term game. He researched different investment options, diversified his portfolio, and held onto his investments for the long haul.

By following these steps, Alex was able to successfully plan and work towards his long-term financial goals.

After setting his long-term financial goals, Alex began the process of planning to achieve them. He knew that achieving his goals would require a combination of hard work, smart saving and investing, and some sacrifices along the way.

The first step Alex took was to create a detailed plan of action. He set a specific timeline for achieving his goals and broke them down into smaller, manageable steps. For example, if he wanted to save $20,000 for a down payment on a house in three years, he would need to save around $555 per month.

To help him stay on track, Alex set up automatic transfers from his checking account to a separate savings account dedicated to his down payment. He also tracked his progress regularly, making sure he was staying within his budget and adjusting his spending as needed.

Planning for long-term financial goals continued...

Alex also began exploring different investment options to grow his money faster. He read books, talked to financial advisors, and did his own research to find the best options for his goals and risk tolerance.

With his plan in place and his investments growing, Alex was able to achieve his long-term financial goals. He purchased his dream home and felt a sense of pride and accomplishment in knowing he had worked hard and made smart financial decisions to make it happen.

Through his experience, Alex learned that planning, perseverance, and flexibility are key to achieving long-term financial goals. He also found that seeking advice and guidance from experts can be incredibly helpful in making informed decisions about investments and financial planning.

Long-term financial planning is essential for achieving financial stability and success. By setting specific goals, creating a plan, and consistently sticking to it, you can build wealth and secure your financial future. It's important to understand that long-term planning is not just for the wealthy or those who are near retirement age. No matter your age or income level, it's crucial to start thinking about your financial future now and take steps to make it happen.

By planning for long-term financial goals, you can prioritize your spending and make informed decisions about where to allocate your money. This can help you avoid unnecessary expenses and focus on what really matters to you. It also allows you to save for important milestones, such as buying a home, starting a family, or pursuing your dream career.

Moreover, long-term financial planning can help you prepare for unexpected events and emergencies. By building up your emergency fund and investing in insurance, you can protect yourself and your loved ones from financial hardships that may arise.

Finally, long-term financial planning helps you achieve a sense of financial security and peace of mind. By creating a clear plan for your future, you can feel confident in your ability to achieve your goals and weather any financial challenges that may come your way.

Chapter 5

Maximizing your paycheck

Maximizing your paycheck means making the most of the income you earn from your job. It involves taking steps to increase your earnings, reduce your expenses, and manage your money wisely so that you can save and invest more effectively.

Here are some ways that Alex used and that you can use to maximize your paycheck:

- **Negotiate your salary:** Alex made sure he was being paid what he was worth by negotiating his salary when starting a new job and during performance reviews.
- **Look for additional income streams:** Alex started a freelance writing gig on the side, which brought in an extra $500 a month.
- **Reduce your expenses:** Alex reviewed his monthly bills and found ways to save money by switching to a cheaper cell phone plan and canceling some subscription services he rarely used.
- **Maximize your benefits:** Alex took full advantage of his employer's benefits, including their 401(k) plan and tuition reimbursement program to finish his college degree.
- **Invest wisely:** Alex diversified his portfolio and put his money into a mix of stocks, bonds, and real estate investment trusts (REITs).

Understanding your paycheck and taxes

Alex was thrilled to have landed a new job as a marketing executive at a top advertising agency. On his first day, he was handed his first paycheck, and he couldn't wait to see how much he would be earning. But when he opened the envelope, he was a little confused by all the numbers and abbreviations on the check.

"Hey, what's all this?" he asked his colleague, who had been with the company for a few years.

"That's your paycheck, buddy," his colleague replied with a smile. "It looks a little intimidating, but it's not as complicated as it seems."

Alex nodded, still a little unsure. His colleague walked him through each section of the paycheck, starting with the gross pay. This was the total amount of money he earned before any taxes or deductions were taken out.

Next, they looked at the deductions section. Here, Alex saw that taxes were being withheld from his paycheck. He noticed the abbreviations FICA and Medicare, which his colleague explained were taxes for Social Security and Medicare programs. Alex also saw a state income tax and federal income tax, both of which were based on his earnings and tax bracket.

After the taxes were deducted, Alex saw a section called pre-tax deductions. This included money he had chosen to put towards his 401(k) retirement account, which would lower his taxable income and help him save for retirement.

Finally, Alex saw a section called net pay, which was the amount of money he would actually take home after all the deductions were taken out.

"Wow, there's a lot to consider!" Alex exclaimed.

His colleague nodded. "It may seem overwhelming at first, but it's important to understand your paycheck so you know what you're earning and how much is being taken out for taxes and other benefits. You can also adjust your pre-tax deductions if you want to contribute more or less to your 401(k) account."

Alex felt more informed and confident in understanding his paycheck. He realized that although the numbers on his paycheck may look confusing, they were all necessary for him to receive his pay, pay his taxes, and contribute to his benefits.

Understanding your paycheck and taxes continued...

Here's a breakdown of the different items you might find on a paycheck, along with a brief explanation of each:

Gross Pay

- The total amount of money you earned before any taxes or deductions are taken out.

Taxes

- Federal Income Tax: A tax on your earnings that goes to the federal government.
- State Income Tax: A tax on your earnings that goes to your state government.
- FICA (Federal Insurance Contributions Act) Tax: A tax that goes towards Social Security and Medicare programs.

Pre-tax Deductions

- 401(k) or Other Retirement Contributions: Money you choose to contribute to a retirement savings account, which reduces your taxable income.

Post-tax Deductions

- Health Insurance Premiums: The amount you pay for health insurance through your employer.
- Other Benefit Contributions: Deductions for other benefits you may receive, such as life insurance or disability insurance.

Net Pay

- The amount of money you actually take home after all taxes and deductions are taken out.

It's important to note that the specific deductions and amounts on a paycheck can vary depending on your employer and your individual situation. It's always a good idea to review your paycheck regularly to make sure everything looks correct and to ask your employer or HR department if you have any questions or concerns.

Strategies for increasing your income

Alex had been working at his job as a marketing executive for a few months and was starting to get into the swing of things. He enjoyed his job and felt like he was making a difference, but he had recently learned that his rent was going up next month. He knew this was going to put a strain on his budget, so he started thinking of ways to increase his income.

One strategy Alex used to increase his income was to ask his boss for a raise. He felt like he had been doing a good job and was adding value to the company, so he scheduled a meeting with his boss to discuss a possible pay increase. During the meeting, he presented his case for why he felt he deserved a raise and highlighted some of his recent accomplishments. His boss was impressed with Alex's work and agreed to a modest pay increase, which would help him cover some of his added expenses.

Another strategy Alex used was to look for freelance work in his spare time. He had some experience in graphic design and knew he could use those skills to create logos and marketing materials for small businesses. He signed up for a few freelance websites and started bidding on projects. Within a few weeks, he had secured a few projects that paid well and didn't take up too much of his free time.

Alex also decided to sell some of his belongings that he no longer used. He had a collection of vinyl records that he had inherited from his grandfather, but he rarely listened to them anymore. He researched the value of his collection and listed them for sale online. Within a few days, he had sold most of his collection for a decent price.

Finally, Alex decided to pick up some extra hours at work. His company had a few upcoming projects that required some overtime work, and Alex volunteered to help out. The extra hours would result in extra income, which would help him cover his added expenses.

In the end, Alex was able to successfully increase his income through a combination of strategies. He negotiated a pay increase, found freelance work, sold some of his belongings, and picked up extra hours at work. With these added sources of income, he was able to cover his added expenses and maintain his financial stability.

Here's a breakdown of the strategies Alex used to increase his income, along with some pros and cons of each:

Ask for a raise

- Pro: Potentially higher income without having to take on additional work

Strategies for increasing your income continued...

- Con: May not be successful, could strain the relationship with your boss
- Example: Alex asked for a raise to help cover his increased rent expenses

Freelance work

- Pro: Can be done on your own time, potentially higher income if successful
- Con: May be difficult to find consistent work, can be time-consuming
- Example: Alex used his graphic design skills to find freelance work on various platforms

Sell belongings

- Pro: Quick way to make money, can help declutter your space
- Con: May not be a sustainable source of income, could regret selling items in the future
- Example: Alex sold his collection of vinyl records to help cover his increased expenses

Pick up extra hours at work

- Pro: Guaranteed source of income, may be easier to get than freelance work
- Con: Could lead to burnout, may not be an option depending on the job
- Example: Alex volunteered to work overtime at his job to increase his income

Overall, it's important to remember that the strategies used to increase income will vary depending on individual circumstances. In Alex's case, he needed to increase his income to cover his increased rent expenses.

40 ways to make an extra income today.

"Freelance work"	Doing odd jobs for neighbors or friends	Renting out photography equipment	Selling stock photos or videos
"Selling goods or services online"	House-sitting for people on vacation	Renting out a parking space or driveway	Designing websites or apps for others
"Participating in the gig economy"	Selling handmade goods on Etsy	Renting out tools or equipment	Creating and selling physical products
"Starting a side business"	Taking paid surveys online	Becoming an influencer on social media	Doing transcription work
"Investing in the stock market or real estate"	Driving for food delivery services like DoorDash or Grubhub	Doing voice-over work for videos or commercials	Doing data entry work
Renting out a spare room on Airbnb	Creating and selling digital products like ebooks or printables	Becoming a paid online content creator	Working as a personal shopper or stylist
Renting out your car on Turo	Creating and selling online courses	Offering consulting services	Offering resume writing or career coaching services
Teaching or tutoring on the side	Working as a virtual assistant	Renting out your boat or water sports equipment	Working as a personal trainer or fitness instructor
Taking on a part-time job	Babysitting	Doing freelance writing or editing work	Renting out space in your home for storage
Pet-sitting or dog-walking	Doing yard work for others	Offering social media management services	Offering cleaning or organizing services

Saving for retirement

Saving for retirement means putting aside money so that you can enjoy your life after you stop working. It helps ensure that you have enough money to pay for the things you need and want, like food, housing, and healthcare, and also gives you the freedom to pursue your interests and hobbies without worrying about money. It's important to save for retirement because you never know what unexpected expenses or challenges you may face in the future, and having a retirement savings plan in place can help you handle them without added stress or financial strain.

Alex was 25 years old and had just started his first full-time job with a salary of $50,000. His employer offered a 401(k) plan with a 50% match up to 6% of his salary. He decided to enroll in the 401(k) plan and contribute 6% of his salary, which amounted to $3,000 per year. He also opened a Roth IRA and contributed an additional $3,000 per year, bringing his total retirement savings to $6,000 per year.

Fast forward 30 years and Alex is now 55 years old and approaching retirement. He's been contributing to his retirement savings consistently over the years and has made smart investment decisions along the way. His 401(k) plan has grown to $500,000 and his Roth IRA has grown to $300,000, for a total of $800,000 in retirement savings.

Alex decides to retire at age 60, which is earlier than the traditional retirement age of 65. He's able to do so comfortably because of his diligent retirement savings plan. He starts receiving Social Security benefits at age 62 and receives $1,500 per month, which supplements his retirement savings.

Alex and his wife decide to travel during their retirement years and visit places they've always wanted to see. They also spend time with their grandchildren and pursue their hobbies. They don't have to worry about financial struggles because of the retirement savings plan they put in place 30 years ago.

Looking back, Alex is grateful for the decision he made to start saving for retirement early in his career. He's able to enjoy his retirement years without the stress of financial worries and is able to live the life he's always dreamed of.

When it comes to saving for retirement, there are different options you can consider, such as:

Retirement accounts through your employer: Some jobs offer retirement plans that let you set aside a portion of your paycheck to invest in the stock market or other investments.

Saving for retirement continued...

The money you put in these accounts is tax-free, so it can grow faster over time. Plus, some employers match your contributions, which means you get free money to help your savings grow even faster!

Individual retirement accounts (IRAs): These are like savings accounts you can open on your own at a bank or investment company. You can choose between a traditional IRA or a Roth IRA, which have different tax benefits. With a traditional IRA, you don't pay taxes on the money you put in until you withdraw it in retirement. With a Roth IRA, you pay taxes on the money you put in now, but you don't pay taxes on it when you withdraw it in retirement.

Health savings accounts (HSAs): These accounts are for medical expenses, but they can also be a good way to save for retirement. If you have a high-deductible health plan, you can put pre-tax money into an HSA and use it to pay for medical expenses. Once you turn 65, you can use the money for anything you want, without paying a penalty.

Pensions: Some jobs offer pensions, which are retirement plans that promise you a certain amount of money each month when you retire. These are less common these days, but they can still be a good option if your employer offers them.

Regular investment accounts: You can also invest your money in regular accounts, like a brokerage account or a savings account. These don't have the same tax benefits as retirement accounts, but they can still be a good way to save for your future.

The amount you need to save for retirement depends on your goals and lifestyle. While it's good to start saving early, don't worry if you can't save a lot right now. Every little bit helps, and you can always increase your contributions later on. It's important to choose a reputable financial institution that has low fees and a good selection of investment options. You can also talk to a financial advisor if you need help making decisions about your retirement savings.

Here's a list investment brokers/ firms to give you a starting point:

Firm Name	Description
Vanguard	Offers a variety of low-cost mutual funds and ETFs, and has a strong reputation for investor-friendly policies.
Fidelity	Provides a range of investment options, including mutual funds, ETFs, and individual stocks, with a user-friendly platform.

Charles Schwab	Has a large selection of investment options and a user-friendly platform, with a strong reputation for excellent customer service.
Robinhood	A popular platform for commission-free trading of stocks, ETFs, and cryptocurrencies, with a user-friendly app.
TD Ameritrade	Provides a range of investment options, including stocks, bonds, mutual funds, and ETFs, with a user-friendly platform and excellent customer service.
E*TRADE	Offers a variety of investment options, including stocks, bonds, mutual funds, and ETFs, with a user-friendly platform and excellent research tools.
Merrill Edge	Offers a wide range of investment options, including stocks, bonds, mutual funds, and ETFs, with a user-friendly platform and access to Merrill Lynch research.
Ally Invest	Provides a range of investment options, including stocks, options, and ETFs, with a user-friendly platform and competitive pricing.
Betterment	Offers a range of automated investment portfolios, with a user-friendly platform and low fees.
Wealthfront	Provides a range of automated investment portfolios, with a user-friendly platform and low fees.

When it comes to trading websites, there are a lot of options out there, some of which offer "free" trades while others charge a fee per trade. It's important to do your research and compare the pros and cons of each type of platform.

With free trading platforms, the main advantage is obviously the lack of fees. However, these platforms may not have as many investment options or research tools as their paid counterparts. Additionally, some free trading platforms may actually make money by selling order flow data to market makers, potentially resulting in less favorable trade execution for the user.

On the other hand, paid trading platforms typically offer more investment options and research tools, as well as better trade execution. However, the fees can add up, especially if you are a frequent trader. It's important to consider your trading habits and investment goals when deciding which type of platform is right for you.

Remember that investing comes with risks, so it's important to have a plan and not invest money you can't afford to lose. Be careful of scams too!

Conclusions

Final thoughts on budgeting

Alex had come a long way since his early days of working at the grocery store. His consistent saving and investment habits had allowed him to build a comfortable life for himself and his family. At age 35, he had a net worth of $500,000, which he had achieved through disciplined saving and investing.

Alex had been careful with his spending, ensuring that he always kept within his budget. He had been able to purchase a larger home and a new car, thanks to his strong credit score and the down payments he was able to make from his savings. Alex was also able to take his family on vacations to new destinations each year, making sure to keep his spending in check while still creating unforgettable memories with his loved ones.

His investment portfolio was diverse, with a mix of stocks, bonds, and real estate investments. Alex had taken the time to research and understand each investment before committing his money to them. His investments had generated significant returns over the years, helping him to grow his wealth steadily.

Alex's financial stability had allowed him to pursue his passions outside of work. He had started his own small business, which he had always dreamed of, and was now generating a healthy profit. His business also allowed him to contribute to his community and give back through various charitable causes.

While Alex knew that he still had a long way to go before he could consider himself financially independent, he was proud of the progress he had made so far. He had been able to achieve his goals through careful planning, smart investments, and disciplined spending habits.

In the end, at the age of 40, Alex has continued to prioritize his budgeting and saving habits. His retirement accounts have grown to a total of $800,000, thanks to consistent contributions and smart investments over the years. He also has a brokerage account with a balance of $200,000, which he uses to diversify his investments.

Alex's net worth has also seen a significant increase. He now owns a spacious house worth $600,000, which he purchased with a sizable down payment, allowing him to keep his monthly mortgage payments in line with his budget. He also recently bought a new car for $35,000, paid in full with cash he had saved over the years.

But Alex's success isn't just measured by his finances. He's also been able to take time off work to travel and explore new places, something he's always been passionate about. He's been able to provide for his family and contribute to their education funds, and he feels confident about their future.

Looking back, Alex knows that his budgeting skills and financial discipline played a significant role in getting him to where he is today. He's grateful for the lessons he's learned and the decisions he's made, and he's excited to see where the future will take him.

Here are Alex's thoughts on budgeting:

- Budgeting helps you gain control over your finances and make progress towards your financial goals.
- It's important to be honest with yourself about your spending habits and to track your expenses regularly to see where your money is going.
- Setting up automatic savings and investing contributions can make it easier to save for your future without even thinking about it.
- Budgeting doesn't have to be restrictive or boring - you can still have fun and enjoy life while living within your means.
- By sticking to a budget, you can avoid the stress and anxiety that comes with living paycheck to paycheck or not knowing where your money is going.
- Learning to budget at a young age can set you up for a lifetime of financial success and security.

Encouragement to continue budgeting

Budgeting can teach you consistency in managing your money, which can lead to all the wonderful benefits mentioned above. By consistently setting aside money for savings, investments, and paying off debts, you can slowly but surely grow your wealth over time. Just like in the examples given, starting small and consistently saving or investing can compound into significant gains over the years. And the discipline and habits developed through budgeting can spill over into other areas of your life, helping you achieve success and reach your goals. So don't underestimate the power of budgeting and the impact it can have on your financial future!

Here are 10 examples of how starting small and compounding with consistency over time can turn into huge payoffs:

Retirement savings: Saving a small amount of money consistently over time can lead to a significant nest egg at retirement age, thanks to the power of compounding interest.

Investing in stocks: Investing a small amount of money in stocks and reinvesting any dividends can lead to significant long-term gains, as the value of the stock and the dividends compound over time.

Paying off debt: Making consistent, on-time payments on debt, even if they are small, can lead to significant progress in paying off the debt over time and ultimately becoming debt-free.

Encouragement to continue budgeting continued....

Building an emergency fund: Saving a small amount of money each month can add up over time and result in a substantial emergency fund that can help cover unexpected expenses without having to rely on credit cards or loans.

Starting a business: Starting a small business and consistently reinvesting profits can lead to significant growth over time and potentially even turn into a large, successful company.

Learning a new skill: Consistently dedicating time and effort to learning a new skill, even if it's just a few hours a week, can lead to significant growth and mastery over time.

Physical fitness: Consistently exercising and making small improvements over time can lead to significant gains in overall health and fitness.

Building a network: Consistently networking and building relationships over time can lead to valuable connections and opportunities down the line.

Writing a book: Consistently dedicating time to writing a book, even if it's just a few pages a day, can lead to a finished manuscript over time.

Learning a new language: Consistently practicing a new language for just a few minutes a day can lead to significant progress over time and potentially even fluency in the language.

Encouragement to continue budgeting continued....

In conclusion, budgeting is a skill that can have a profound impact on one's financial life. By taking control of your spending, saving consistently, and investing wisely, you can achieve financial freedom and security. It's not always easy, but the discipline and consistency that come with budgeting can help you turn small actions into big results over time. So, start small, stay consistent, and watch your financial future grow.

Many successful people have started their lives with little or nothing and through hard work, perseverance, and dedication, they have achieved great success. These individuals have made significant contributions to society and have inspired countless others to follow in their footsteps. In this list, we'll explore the stories of ten real-world people who overcame adversity to make a lasting impact on the world around them.

Oprah Winfrey - media executive, actress, talk show host, and philanthropist who overcame a difficult childhood to become one of the most influential women in the world.

J.K. Rowling - author of the Harry Potter series, who went from living on welfare to becoming one of the best-selling authors of all time.

Richard Branson - founder of the Virgin Group, who started with a small record store and went on to build a global conglomerate.

Elon Musk - founder of Tesla, SpaceX, and other cutting-edge technology companies, who started with little more than a dream and a determination to make it happen.

Encouragement to continue budgeting continued....

Arianna Huffington - co-founder of the Huffington Post, who started her career as a political commentator and went on to become one of the most successful media entrepreneurs in the world.

Steve Jobs - co-founder of Apple, who started his career in a garage and went on to revolutionize the tech industry with his innovative products.

Tony Robbins - motivational speaker and author, who overcame a difficult childhood and became one of the most sought-after speakers in the world.

Mark Cuban - entrepreneur and investor, who started with a small software company and went on to become a billionaire through his investments in tech and other industries.

Michael Jordan - retired professional basketball player, who started with humble beginnings and went on to become one of the greatest athletes of all time.

Vera Wang - fashion designer, who started her career as a figure skater and went on to become one of the most successful fashion designers in the world.

Simon Cowell - music executive and television producer, who started as a talent scout and went on to become one of the most influential people in the music and television industries.

Tyler Perry - actor, writer, and producer, who overcame a difficult childhood and went on to become one of the most successful filmmakers in the world.

Encouragement to continue budgeting continued....

Ursula Burns - business executive, who grew up in a housing project in New York City and went on to become the first black female CEO of a Fortune 500 company.

Colonel Sanders - founder of KFC, who started his business in his 60s and went on to become one of the most successful entrepreneurs of all time.

Warren Buffett - investor and philanthropist, who started with a small investment in a textile company and went on to become one of the wealthiest people in the world.

Ray Kroc - founder of McDonald's, who started as a struggling milkshake machine salesman and went on to build one of the most successful fast-food franchises in history.

Martha Stewart - media personality and businesswoman, who started as a model and went on to become one of the most successful entrepreneurs in the home and lifestyle industries.

Dwayne "The Rock" Johnson - actor and former professional wrestler, who started with nothing and went on to become one of the most successful entertainers in the world.

Jeff Bezos - founder of Amazon, who started with a small online bookstore and went on to build one of the largest e-commerce companies in the world.

Jay-Z - rapper, entrepreneur, and philanthropist, who overcame a difficult childhood and went on to become one of the most successful and influential musicians in the world.

In conclusion, the key to success in life is consistency and delayed gratification. It's easy to give in to instant pleasures and spend money recklessly, but those who are able to resist those temptations and make wise financial decisions are the ones who will thrive in the long run. Alex and the people mentioned above all started with nothing but through hard work, dedication, and smart financial choices, they were able to make a significant impact in the world. It's never too early or too late to start making those choices for yourself. So start today, stay consistent, and watch as your future self thanks you for it. Let's go!

Peace and Power my friend,

Made in the USA
Columbia, SC
15 March 2025

55204459R00024